A souvenir guide

Hindhead Common and the Devil's Punch Bowl

Surrey

GW00645291

❈ National Trust

Hindhead: An Epic Evolution

Made up of the Devil's Punch Bowl and Hindhead Common, Hindhead is a magnificent wilderness offering unrivalled distant views, fantastic walks and providing a precious wildlife haven.

Poor soil and harsh, windswept conditions created this bleak, sparsely inhabited landscape. So it is perhaps surprising that Hindhead has such a colourful story to tell.

The fable of Thor

There is an ancient myth to explain the unusual hook-shape of the Devil's Punch Bowl valley. It is said that the Devil lived in the three hills nearby, known as the 'Devil's Jumps', and that Thor, the god of thunder, lived in Thor's Leah (Thursley). The Devil enjoyed tormenting Thor by constantly jumping between his hills. One day, in exasperation, Thor retaliated by picking up a huge scoop of earth to throw at the Devil, creating the unique shape of this valley.

It was actually formed by springs emerging where porous sandstone meets impervious clay underneath.

Above Walkers enjoying a stroll through Hindhead Common

Above right George Mayes, the Punch Bowl's milkman, outside the broomsquires' cottages in 1907

'One of the wildest, sweetest spots in England.'

Anne Gilchrist,
writer and Haslemere resident

Commons and common land

From Norman times, land with soil too poor to cultivate became known as 'manorial waste'. The lord of the manor, which was sometimes the Church, granted tenants certain 'rights', called commoners' rights, over these areas which became known as common land. Rights were quite particular, typically allowing a fixed number of a specified animal, usually sheep or pigs, to graze, or a fixed amount of a commodity, such as firewood, stone or bracken (for animal bedding), to be taken each year.

Hindhead Common and the Devil's Punch Bowl were common land and owned by the powerful and immensely wealthy Bishops of Winchester. The bishops had vast land holdings in Hampshire and Surrey, and Farnham Castle was one of their main residences for 800 years.

The Devil's Punch Bowl and Hindhead Common

A system of small fields in the valley is thought to have Saxon origins, and the few farms here once supported a meagre, isolated living. The western Punch Bowl hillside is woodland. Hindhead Common remains almost entirely open heathland.

Broomsquires once ran a local industry making brooms from birch and heather, selling their wares at London and Portsmouth markets. As late as 1900, nine local families were known to be cutting birch saplings here for broom-making.

A vital route

These lonely hills sit directly between London and Portsmouth. For as long as there has been a road linking these two cities it has passed over the top of Hindhead, because going round it would add a long detour.

Known as the Portsmouth Road, it has been centre-stage throughout Hindhead's varied history.

The Portsmouth Road

Ever since Henry VIII commissioned the ill-fated Mary Rose in 1509, Portsmouth has been an important naval base, making a road linking it to London essential. Halfway between the two, Hindhead's steep, lonely hills were a major obstacle and made this a notoriously difficult and much-feared route.

The sharp incline from the north presented the greatest challenges. Horses often became tired out by the difficult climb.

Worse, isolated and often shrouded in mist, this part of the road was a favourite haunt of robbers and highwaymen.

Until 1600, the road passed through the villages of Liphook and Thursley. As Portsmouth's naval importance increased, a more direct route was built south of Thursley and the Red Lion Inn established itself on the new road. Travellers would stop here before embarking on the next treacherous stage of their journey, often hoping they could find others to join. As you will discover on pages 6 and 7, this did not always end well.

Turnpike Trusts

By the early 18th century, the increase in wheeled vehicles had caused serious deterioration in road surfaces. So Parliament allowed Turnpike Trusts to maintain them under licence and to charge tolls. The Portsmouth Road was run by the Kingston-upon-Thames to Sheet Bridge Turnpike Company from 1749 to 1873.

Left J.M.W. Turner's sketch, made into this engraving in 1808, portrays Hindhead as forbidding and barren. And in 1822, the author William Cobbett denounced Hindhead as 'certainly the most villainous spot that God ever made' after his guide lost their way in fog

Right The Portsmouth Road round the Punch Bowl *c.* 1900

'Quite sterile, given up to barrenness, horrid and frightful to look on, not only good for little, but good for nothing.'

Author Daniel Defoe (?1661–1731) describes Hindhead in *A tour through the whole island of Great Britain* (c. 1724–1727)

A feat of engineering

Over the years, carriages got so much heavier that by the 1820s it was necessary to construct a lower 'coach road' round the Punch Bowl. This would prevent coach-horses becoming exhausted by the climb from Thursley and making their passengers easy targets for thieves.

The turnpike company hired hundreds of labourers who dug through a section of the eastern hillside and used horse-drawn carts to transport the earth away. The upper route was left as a track and is now the byway from our main car park towards Gibbet Hill. The new coach road remained the route of the Portsmouth Road until the A3 tunnel opened in 2011 (see page 28).

Milestones

Although not compulsory on British roads until 1767, milestones in a form that we might recognise today date back to the Romans, who measured distance on their new roads using stone cylinders or pillars.

At their peak, milestones featured on 20,000 miles of UK roads, but only 9,000 or so still exist. Many were removed or defaced in the Second World War to confuse potential invaders.

An original milestone was found in the Punch Bowl's undergrowth. It has been reinstated along the old Portsmouth Road, now known as Byway 500, in almost exactly the place it would have occupied before the 1820s. The milestone near Boundless Road car park is a replica.

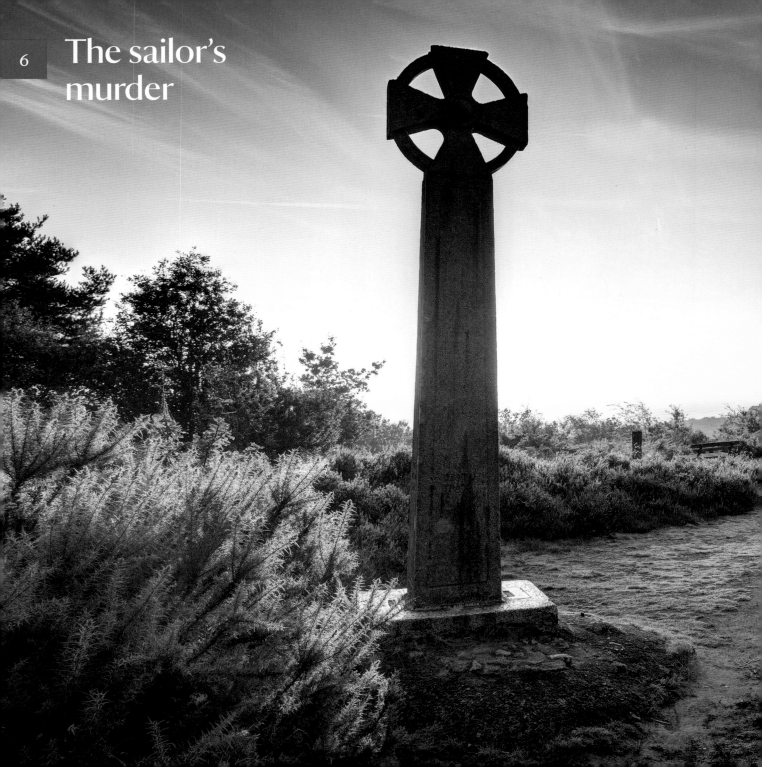

The sailor's murder

The Celtic Cross stands at the top of Gibbet Hill. The Latin inscription in its base translates to 'Light after darkness. Peace is passing away. Hope in light. Salvation after death.'

In 1786, Hindhead Common was the scene of an infamous murder. On 24 September, a sailor en-route to Portsmouth stopped at the Red Lion Inn in Thursley, where he was befriended by three men. The sailor generously paid for his new friends' drinks with a golden guinea – earned on his last sea voyage.

He continued on his journey but was ruthlessly set upon by the three men on Hindhead Common, who robbed him and cut his throat. The perpetrators were apprehended within hours at the Sun Inn in Rake, about five miles south along the Portsmouth Road, where they were selling their victim's clothes.

Harsh justice
Haslemere Justice of the Peace, the Reverend James Fielding, committed the three men to trial at Kingston Assizes. Within six months they had been convicted and sentenced to death. Ironically Fielding was thought to be a highwayman or a receiver of their spoils.

Two days after sentencing, the men – Michael Casey, Edward Lonegon, and James Marshall – were hanged at the top of Hindhead Hill, near the scene of the crime. Their bodies were then tarred and put in metal and chain cages in which they were suspended from a specially built, 10-metre (30-foot) wooden gibbet. Perhaps as a warning to other local villains, gruesomely they were left hanging in their cages to rot for three years.

The Celtic Cross and Sailor's Stone
As a result, local people considered Hindhead Hill, which has been known as Gibbet Hill ever since, not only dangerous but haunted as well, and would not go there. Eventually in 1851 Sir William Erle of nearby Bramshott erected an imposing granite cross with a Celtic design to help dispel local fears. This still dominates the top of the hill.

Although the sailor's identity has never been confirmed, he is thought to be Edward Hardman. His body was buried at Thursley church. A local man, James Stillwell, had a handsome memorial stone made in his honour and placed at the spot of this barbarous murder and brutal retribution. It can now be seen on Byway 500.

The curse
The back of the sailor's memorial stone reads 'cursed be the man who moveth or injureth this stone'. But in 1826, it was moved to the new lower coach road, near Gibbet Hill. Local people believed Stillwell's nephew put a curse on the headstone because he disliked the Turnpike Trust's choice of location. The curse is said to have struck workmen who moved the stone in 1831 and in 1889: one was badly injured and another met an untimely death. The National Trust has no plans to move this headstone again!

Above *The Deed* by an unknown artist. The sailor's ruthless murder has been a source of material for many artists and writers, and is even mentioned in Charles Dickens's *Nicholas Nickleby*

The railway and the writers

In 1859 the London to Portsmouth railway was completed, transforming the fortunes of this area.

Hindhead's hills had again proved a serious obstacle as the ascent from the east was so steep the line had to divert south through Haslemere. Regardless, the seven miles of continuous incline meant every train had to stop there. The journey from Waterloo to Haslemere, even then, took about an hour.

The arrival of the railway ended the area's isolation and economic decline. It also offered a safer, more comfortable alternative to coach journeys over Hindhead hill. So by the 1870s the coaching trade through Hindhead had vanished – and with it the robbers and highwaymen. Soon, far from being seen as a desolate and eerie place, Hindhead was praised for its clean air and spectacular scenery.

With the Industrial Revolution bringing new forms of employment in the cities, London's population expanded rapidly. It became over-crowded, dirty and often foul-smelling. Newly accessible by train, rural Hindhead was attractive to those who needed access to London but no longer wished to live there, especially writers.

Below The station decorated to honour a visit by King Edward VII on 3 November 1903. The King was visiting to lay the foundation stone of King Edward VII hospital at Midhurst; he travelled as far as Haslemere by train and took a Landau (a type of enclosed, horse-drawn carriage) the rest of the way. This photo was taken when he came to catch the train back to London

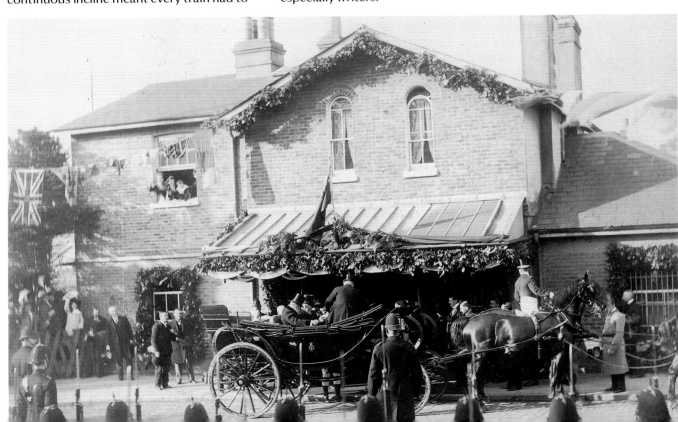

The Hill-top writers

Alfred, Lord Tennyson 1809–1892
Although he didn't come from London, some credit Alfred, Lord Tennyson, who was made Poet Laureate in 1850, with leading the writers' migration to Hindhead. He moved here from the Isle of Wight in 1867, having grown frustrated with tourists seeking him out at Farringford, his home there. He rented Grayshott Hall (then Grayshott Farm) while he found a secluded plot of land at Black Down. It was there he built Aldworth as his summer residence.

Anne Gilchrist 1828–1885
Anne published several works including a biography of Mary Lamb. She was a key member of the Hindhead literary circle and entertained William and Christina Rossetti as well as Lord Tennyson at her rented property, Brookbank, in Shottermill. Anne showed Tennyson and his wife Emily the area personally and persuaded them to move here.

Anne, a widow, is probably best known for her 'one-sided courtship' of the poet Walt Whitman. In 1876, she moved to Philadelphia to be near him. Sadly for Anne, Walt never reciprocated her feelings, but their meeting was the start of a life-long friendship.

Sir Arthur Conan Doyle 1859–1930
Sir Arthur came to live in Hindhead in 1898 in the hope that its clean air would help his wife's failing health. He built Undershaw just west of Hindhead Crossroads and it was here that he wrote one of his most famous Sherlock Holmes novels, *The Hound of the Baskervilles*, in 1901. He took an active part in village life, playing in both the cricket and football teams.

Sir Arthur's wife died in 1906, after which he remarried and moved away.

Other Hindhead writers
Following Anne Gilchrist's return to London, in 1871 George Eliot, also known as Marian Evans, rented Brookbank to complete her novel, *Middlemarch*. The playwright George Bernard Shaw briefly lived at Blen Cathra in Hindhead, now the site of St Edmund's School, and Flora Thompson, author of *Lark Rise to Candleford*, worked in Grayshott's post office around this time.

Left Alfred, Lord Tennyson was Poet Laureate for 42 years. He was so successful in the role that when he died in 1892 the position wasn't filled for four years because he seemed irreplaceable

Below left Anne Gilchrist by Herbert Harlakenden Gilchrist (1857–1914). Anne's first publication was a biography of William Blake, which she finished for her husband following his death

Below right Before Sir Arthur Conan Doyle joined the local cricket team, he played for Marylebone Cricket Club. An occasional bowler, he took just one first-class wicket in his time, but it was an impressive one – he dismissed W.G. Grace for 110

Rural flight and Whitaker Wright

'For a time everything he touched turned – or seemed to turn – to gold. The name of Whitaker Wright became a synonym for success and magnificence.'

The Daily Telegraph, January 1904

The Industrial Revolution encouraged country dwellers to seek employment in the cities. Rural areas lost people making a living from the land and the use of commoners' rights gradually declined. However commons became open spaces enjoyed by many.

Prompted by the rapidly increasing population, the 1845 Enclosures Act allowed land owners to fence commons off if there were development prospects, and to sell them for building.

By now Hindhead Common and the Devil's Punch Bowl were part of South Park Farm, immediately south-east of Hindhead, but they had not been enclosed.

Wright at Lea Park

In about 1890 an exceptionally wealthy financier, Whitaker Wright, acquired South Park Farm and the adjacent estate, Lea Park. Wright had made his fortune in mining, raising the necessary finance by issuing bonds in his companies. He was a flamboyant man for whom it was important to show off his successes. He set about transforming his new estates to impress society guests and potential investors, adding extravagant new wings to the main house and landscaping the gardens. His grand schemes provided work for many people in nearby Witley, but he upset Haslemere residents by plundering the commons for trees and shrubs for his gardens. But in 1902 events took an unexpected turn.

Above Lea Park as seen from the South West. Sadly the mansion was gutted by fire in 1952 and little remains today

A spectacular fall from grace

A downturn in mining drove Wright to resort to some highly dubious practices to fulfil his obligations to bond holders; he was accused of misusing investors' funds and some lost their entire capital stake. Ultimately an arrest warrant for fraud was issued. Tipped off, he fled to New York using a false identity, but was apprehended on arrival and eventually extradited.

Wright faced trial at the Old Bailey in late 1903 and on 26 January 1904 he was found guilty and sentenced to a jail term. Unable to face life behind bars, or its consequences, he took a cyanide capsule that he had hidden from court officials and died in rooms below the court.

Whitaker Wright was revered in Witley for the work he had brought in hard times. Local people lined the route of his funeral cortège to All Saints' Church in Witley to pay their last respects.

An uncertain future

The Lea Park estate had to be sold. The 300 hectares (750 acres) of common land that comprised Hindhead Common and the Devil's Punch Bowl were offered as a separate auction lot.

There was great anxiety about the future of these commons. The easy access to London brought by the railway made them an attractive development prospect, likely to be lost as a treasured open space.

Fortunately one of the founders of a new charity, the National Trust, lived in Haslemere. He was Sir Robert Hunter.

Above Wright at his trial

Left Wright in more prosperous times

Sir Robert Hunter

Sir Robert Hunter was a co-founder of the National Trust. He was also a Haslemere resident.

In 1867, aged just 23, the academically brilliant Robert Hunter became lawyer to the Commons Preservation Society after submitting one of the best entries for an essay writing competition on ways to save common land for the public. This marked the start of his life-long dedication to protecting open spaces.

The Commons Preservation Society

In 1865 Liberal MP George Shaw-Lefevre set up the Commons Preservation Society (now the Open Spaces Society). He had realised the extent to which the Enclosures Acts had allowed landlords to sell off common land for development, with commons near cities most vulnerable. In his role, Robert Hunter became an expert in common land law and successfully fought to save various commons, including Wimbledon and Epping Forest.

Later career

Robert Hunter was appointed Solicitor to the General Post Office in 1882, a pre-eminent government role for which he was knighted in 1894. But he never allowed the demands of this job to limit his dedication to saving common land. The Hunter family moved to Three Gates Lane, Haslemere in 1882, where Sir Robert lived for the rest of his life.

Sir Robert retired in July 1913 but died of septicaemia on 6 November the same year. Unusually for a devout man he chose to be buried in an unmarked grave, but St Bartholomew's Church, Haslemere has a memorial plaque to him.

Forming the National Trust

Over the years, it became clear to Robert that an organisation was needed which could acquire open spaces for the benefit of the public. As early as 1884 he had developed a concept of a 'national trust', but it was not until 1895 that the National Trust was formally established. Although Octavia Hill and Canon Hardwicke Rawnsley were also founders of today's National Trust, it was Robert Hunter, the least conspicuous, who was legal architect, mastermind, and its first Chairman.

Acquiring Hindhead

In the early years the Trust acquired only modest holdings. When the opportunity to acquire the common land at Hindhead and the Devil's Punch Bowl arose in 1905, Sir Robert, highly respected

Above Robert Hunter as a young man

Left Sir Robert's Three Gates Lane House in about 1884

Opposite The first page of the 1907 National Trust Act

locally, approached the Haslemere Commons Preservation Society. They raised £3,625, successfully bid for this land and, gave it to the National Trust early the following year. This huge area of open space in the heart of south-east England owned on behalf of the public transformed the Trust's fortunes and firmly established the charity. Further gifts of land and money swiftly followed.

The National Trust Act

This acquisition also prompted Sir Robert, demonstrating immense foresight, to make sure the Trust could never be pressurised to part with its property. He wrote the National Trust Act to set in law that we must hold our land in perpetuity. Passed in 1907, it remains the feature which distinguishes us from other charities.

[7 Edw. 7.]   *National Trust Act, 1907.*   [Ch. cxxxvi.]

CHAPTER cxxxvi.

An Act to incorporate and confer powers upon the A.D. 1907.
National Trust for Places of Historic Interest or
Natural Beauty.   [21st August, 1907.]

WHEREAS the National Trust for Places of Historic Interest or Natural Beauty (hereinafter referred to as "the Association") was in the year 1894 incorporated as an Association not for profit under the Companies Acts 1862 to 1890 with a liability of the members limited by guarantee :

And whereas the Association was incorporated for the purposes of promoting the permanent preservation for the benefit of the nation of lands and tenements (including buildings) of beauty or historic interest and as regards lands for the preservation (so far as practicable) of their natural aspect features and animal and plant life :

And whereas the Association in furtherance of those purposes have acquired considerable property comprising common park and mountain land and buildings and are or are reputed to be the owners of or interested in the properties specified in the First Schedule to this Act to the extent and in the manner therein specified :

And whereas the public are admitted to the enjoyment of the lands buildings and property held by the Association but no adequate powers exist for regulating the use of or protecting the property of the Association or for controlling the persons using the same or resorting thereto :

And whereas with a view to the continuance of the work of the Association for obtaining and preserving lands and buildings as aforesaid and for the permanent holding and maintenance thereof and for the preventing as far as possible their destruction

1

The earliest days

In 1906 the National Trust had neither the means nor the structures to run such a large area of open space. So Sir Robert Hunter set up a committee of volunteers to manage Hindhead Common and the Devil's Punch Bowl, the Hindhead Commons Management Committee. Sir Robert was its Chairman, a Mr William Collins was appointed Keeper and funds came from local donations. Members of the Committee included Sir Arthur Conan Doyle as Honorary Fire Captain.

Minute book records tell us that the first Committee was most concerned about fire, disfigurement of the hillside by unauthorised stone excavation and inappropriate use of vehicles.

Committees of volunteers managed these commons until 1993 when the National Trust found the resources for full-time management. However the Black Down & Hindhead Supporters and the Ludshott Committee continue to advise and raise funds for local Trust properties.

Early acquisitions
Under Sir Robert's stewardship of his Hindhead Commons Management Committee, the Trust rapidly gained huge support in the area. Money raised from local gifts and fundraising efforts allowed the purchase of Ludshott Common in 1908, Marley Common in 1911 and Waggoners Wells in 1919. The latter was in memory of Sir Robert Hunter.

Notable benefactors
Miss Marion James 1833–1910
Miss James was probably the earliest National Trust benefactor other than the founders themselves. In 1908 she gave us Nutcombe Down and Bramshott Chase. She then helped secure the acquisition of Ludshott Common and made a large donation towards it. A walk across Nutcombe Down was named Miss James' Walk in her memory and the footbridge over the new A3 is called Miss James' Bridge.

Above The heathland at Ludshott was acquired with the help of Miss James

Opposite Miss James moved to Grayshott in 1888. As a musician who inherited money from an employer, she was one of the intellectuals attracted to the area once the railway was established. She also contributed substantially to the building of St Luke's Church, Grayshott, where she is buried

Left Professor Tyndall was also a keen mountaineer and was part of the first team to climb the Weisshorn, Switzerland in 1861

Below The Robertson memorial at Hindhead

Professor Tyndall 1820–1893

Professor John Tyndall was a celebrated 19th-century physicist, who is credited with explaining why the sky is blue. He moved to Hindhead in 1883 and built the first large house here, Hindhead House. His presence attracted many others to the area, much to his displeasure. In 1931, his widow gave the woodland west of the A287, now named Tyndall's Wood, to the National Trust.

William Alexander Robertson 1871–1937

William Robertson, a judge, left a substantial legacy to the National Trust in 1937 for the purchase of land or buildings within reach of London.

His gift was in memory of two of his brothers, Norman and Laurance, who were killed in the First World War. He insisted that there should be a memorial to them at each property acquired with his money. His legacy enabled the acquisition of Highcombe Edge, the western ridge of the Punch Bowl. The memorial to his brothers can be seen on the Highcombe Hike route.

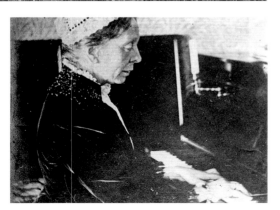

20th-century Hindhead

The main part of the Lea Park estate, which included the house, failed to attract a buyer at the 1905 auction. It languished deserted until 1908 when it was purchased by a Lord Pirrie.

Lord Pirrie was chairman of renowned Belfast ship builders, Harland and Wolff. He was Lord Mayor of Belfast from 1896–8, an Irish Privy Councillor and made Viscount Pirrie in 1921, when he was elected to the new Northern Ireland Senate. Like his Lea Park predecessor, he was attracted to the estate as a means of entertaining and impressing important guests.

The Belvedere

Viscount Pirrie acquired further land to the south of his new estate, re-established an old deer park at Hurt Hill which bordered Hindhead Common and installed fine new wrought-iron gates which each bore the motif of a white crown with the letter 'P' in the centre. The finishing touch to the deer park was an unusual belvedere, a pavilion which he used to host extravagant lunches for his shooting parties. He chose to build this in a remote location, but one with commanding views over his estate, no doubt to underline its magnificence. Known to this day as the Temple of the Four Winds, the pavilion was completed in 1910.

From disuse to disrepair

Viscount Pirrie died in 1924 aged 77 and the estate was sold. The new owner renamed the estate Witley Park, but the belvedere was little used and fell into disrepair.

Hurt Hill was acquired by the National Trust in 1955 thanks to a generous legacy from Mr E.S. Arnold. Sadly by this time the belvedere had been neglected for years. Vandals stole the lead roofing in 1959 and by 1965 it had been declared unsafe. The National Trust had little choice but to dismantle it, leaving just the octagonal base.

Above Lord Pirrie's belvedere c. 1910 at the Temple of the Four Winds

Left Viscount Pirrie with his wife, Margaret Montgomery Carlisle, on a business trip to South America in May 1924. Pirrie died of bronchial pneumonia on this voyage

Opposite Visitors enjoy the restored views from the former site of the belvedere

The unsinkable ship

Harland and Wolff built the RMS Titanic, whose fateful maiden voyage was in April 1912. Lord Pirrie had intended to sail on this exciting Atlantic crossing but was unwell and stayed at home. His nephew, Thomas Andrews, who was Chief Architect to Harland and Wolff, did sail. His actions – reportedly including helping passengers onto lifeboats and throwing deckchairs to those in the water – were credited with saving many lives, but sadly at the cost of his own. His body was never recovered. Perhaps surprisingly, the Titanic tragedy did not significantly damage Harland and Wolff's fortunes and Lord Pirrie remained chairman.

Revealing the past

In 2012 National Trust volunteers excavated the belvedere's stone and tiled base, which had become partly buried. The Black Down & Hindhead Supporters funded extensive scrub clearance to reinstate the views Viscount Pirrie's guests would have admired, and an ongoing project to stabilise the octagonal base.

RAF Gibbet Hill

Although little remains today, an RAF signalling station was based at Gibbet Hill from 1942 to 1958. It consisted of four 76-metre (250-foot) pylon-style wooden masts that were operated from nissen huts underneath which housed the generators, signalling equipment and offices.

Gee whizz

RAF Gibbet Hill was part of a signalling system called 'Gee', which was the cutting edge of technology at the time. It consisted of a main signalling station at RAF Daventry and at least two other 'slave' stations, of which Gibbet Hill was one. By picking up signals from a minimum of three fixed points, pilots could accurately locate their exact position from anywhere over the East of England, transforming their chances of a safe return home. Gibbet Hill would have been an ideal location because of its relatively high altitude and open landscape.

The station pulsed out a regular signal 24 hours a day and was manned by a rota of RAF operators. Including the RAF engineers it was run by a team of about twenty who were billeted in nearby villages.

Below The Gibbet Hill masts were visible for miles around

Opposite below Charles Abbott (1933–2012) with a Vanguard by the Celtic Cross, 1953. He served at RAF Gibbet Hill from 1951–1954 as an Aircraftsman, 1st Class and met his wife – who was training to be an army nurse in Liphook – in Shottermill while stationed here. Charles was also a relief driver for his unit. He described his posting here as 'a time of my life that I look back on with many happy memories'

Tragedy strikes

For all the invaluable guidance it offered to our pilots, RAF Gibbet Hill was to see disaster right at the very end of the War. On 6 May 1945, just two days before the end of the War in Europe was declared, a USA Air Force Curtis C-46D airplane returning injured American servicemen to a US military hospital in Winchester got lost in fog and crashed into one of the masts. Fire broke out and all 22 on board perished. It was a Sunday evening and the station captain, Flight Lieutenant Parish, had sent his staff out to a local pub for the evening, offering to man the radar system himself. Sadly he too died in the fire.

After the War

The RAF maintained their lease on Gibbet Hill and the station continued to operate for some years after the War ended. As late as 1957 the RAF had plans to make Gibbet Hill a permanent station, but by 1958 a newer technology superseded the Gee system and Gibbet Hill was no longer needed. The RAF cleared the site and returned the land to the National Trust the same year.

Only the old fire engine garage survives. It is the concrete-sided structure just south of the main car park. There are plans to renovate it so it can house a permanent record of the RAF's time here.

Left A group of Gibbet Hill airmen. From L–R: Charles Abbott (Radar Mechanic), Pete Singleton (RAF Police), Dave Killingback (Unit Driver) and Bob Bryant (Unit Clerk). We do not know the identity of the fifth man, who was possibly a fireman

Below The Celtic Cross next to one of the Gibbet Hill masts

Flora and Fauna

Hindhead Common is predominantly made up of heathland and woodland.

Heathland

Odd though it seems, wild, open heathland landscapes are man-made. Bronze Age settlers realised that the free-draining sandy soils were not able to support cereal crops, so instead these areas were used for animals to graze and for gathering wood and other raw materials.

Over thousands of years the soil was further impoverished by grazing stock, and by the removal of vegetation such as bracken for animal bedding and heather for thatching and firewood. This meant that over many centuries these sandstone hills became open, windswept landscapes where only the toughest plant species could survive. Hindhead Common and the Devil's Punch Bowl have large areas of heathland which formed in this way.

Heathland plants

The main components of this unique environment are heather, grasses, gorse, bracken and bilberry, and in places, just bare sand. Trees are sparse, mainly birch and pine, with the occasional oak or mountain ash. The heather varieties are mainly common or ling heather, bell heather and cross-leaved heather, while the grasses include purple moor, Yorkshire fog and wavy hair. There are two types of gorse, common gorse and dwarf gorse.

Heathlands are too inhospitable for many rare plant species, but Hindhead Common and the Devil's Punch Bowl boast bog cotton grass, the insect-eating sundew and, in the wetter areas, bog asphodel.

Above **Hindhead supports three species of heather**

Opposite (clockwise from top left)
A sparrowhawk takes a rest

Brimstone butterflies never settle with their wings open

A kestrel hovers

The distinctive adder in heather. They usually only bite when alarmed or disturbed

Heathland wildlife

Considering heathlands support a very limited diversity of plant species, it is surprising that they are such havens for wildlife. Yet many species, particularly birds, reptiles and butterflies, have adapted to, and then become dependent on, these harsh habitats.

Birds

Heathland is very open, so birds of prey, such as sparrowhawks and kestrels, can spot food over a wide expanse. Smaller birds, including nightjars and woodlarks, might favour heathland because they nest on the ground. Others perhaps enjoy the safety offered by thick spiny gorse, for example stonechats and Dartford warblers.

Reptiles

Reptiles like the warmth of sandy soil and most of them hibernate in winter. At Hindhead we see all the UK's common snakes – the adder, smooth snake and grass snake. We also have two species of lizard, the common lizard and the sand lizard. These are all harmless except the adder, which enjoys bathing in the summer sun; watch out for the easily-identifiable zig-zag markings down its back!

Insects

Heathland supports a huge diversity of insects including many species of butterflies, moths and dragonflies. Hindhead enjoys regular sightings of heath, brimstone and large white butterflies as well as occasional sightings of grayling, green hairstreak and silver-studded blue butterflies. In late summer, large, colourful hawker dragonflies are also in evidence.

Loss of heathland

Over the last century almost 90% of the UK's heathlands have been lost. This is because commoners gradually ceased to exercise their rights and stock-grazing died out, and also because land was taken for development.

Over time, scrub woodland, made up largely of pine, birch and holly, encroached on the remaining heathlands. The loss of these open landscapes posed a very serious threat to heathland-dependent wildlife, particularly ground-nesting birds, reptiles and some insect species.

At Hindhead, scrub also obscured some stunning distant views.

Heathland restoration

Today, along with rain forests, heathlands are among the most threatened habitats in the world. But in recent years the National Trust, together with other conservation groups, has introduced a major programme to restore its heathland. Hindhead Common and the Devil's Punch Bowl were some of the first to benefit. Since the mid-1990s large areas lost to scrub woodland have been restored, leaving only a scattering of heathland trees so that large, open areas of heathers, gorse and grasses can re-establish.

Above right **Scrub encroachment is one of the key threats to heathland**

At Hindhead a few Exmoor ponies live on the commons all year, while about forty Highland cattle are free to roam and feed off the heathland in summer.

Some human help too

Hindhead's hard-working volunteers also help us to maintain the heathland, cutting birch and pine saplings as well as overgrown gorse in the winter months. Together with some mechanical cutting, these efforts throw a vital lifeline to the heathland-dependent species whose survival has been threatened by the loss of their habitat.

Special status

The success of this restoration programme has led to large parts of both Hindhead Common and the Devil's Punch Bowl being recognised both as Sites of Special Scientific Interest (SSSI) and Special Protection Areas (SPA, the European designation) for the quality of their heathland. This obliges us to prevent deterioration of this habitat and disturbance of protected and endangered species.

Maintaining heathland

As grazing animals helped create heathlands, it stands to reason that reintroducing them would be the best way to maintain the areas we restored.

Bringing back the animals

Through the centuries, a wide variety of animals have been seen on the common, in particular pigs and sheep. But to make sure our open spaces can safely be enjoyed by everyone, we have introduced ponies and some carefully chosen, very placid, breeds of cattle to help maintain our heaths.

Left A Highland cow grazes at Hindhead

Far left Some of the Exmoor ponies that help maintain Hindhead's heathland

Above Local grazier Sally Scheffers with Hindhead's Head Ranger Matt Cusack. Sally's cattle help maintain the land here

Woodland

The woodland at Hindhead is most prominent on the western slope of the Punch Bowl, at Hurt Hill and at Tyndall's Wood. Like the heathland, it is a haven for wildlife, with pipistrelle bats, tawny owls, goshawks and dormice making these sanctuaries their homes.

Ancient woodland

Much of the woodland on the Punch Bowl slopes and at Hurt Hill is 'ancient', meaning it has been woodland since records began in 1600. It will have been used for timber, with trees regularly coppiced or felled, but never cultivated. This means the woodland floor will have experienced

The woodland today

The wooded sandy-soiled escarpments of Hindhead favour beech, oak, sweet chestnut, birch, larch, and pine, with holly and bilberry forming quite dense undergrowth in places. There are some fine beech trees near the Temple of the Four Winds (on the Hidden Hindhead route) and along the Sailor's Lane (on the Highcombe Hike route).

Productive woodland

These woods once provided timber for construction and fuel. Work in the woodlands was physically demanding. Woodmen processed the timber on site as it was easier to extract planks and beams from the woods than the whole tree trunk and saw-pits were common. Sawyers cut timber with long saws, which required one man at each end.

Coppicing

Some of the woodland areas are dominated by less mature sweet chestnut trees. These areas have been regularly coppiced.

Coppicing is another traditional way of making woodland productive. When certain trees – such as hazel and sweet chestnut – are felled they don't die, but instead rapidly grow new shoots from the remaining stump or 'stool'. Regular coppicing is an effective way of making sure woodland continues to provide a steady supply of useful timber.

The coppicing process

Stems are felled in winter when the sap is in the stump. In spring new shoots will grow from the large root system which has been left in place. The new shoots are allowed to grow for up to 20 years and then harvested again. Each cycle of growth and harvesting is known as a rotation.

Using the timber

Coppiced chestnut has traditionally been used for fencing and roofing tiles. Thinner stems from crops grown on a short rotation were shaped into walking sticks. Charcoal, for furnaces, was made from off-cuts.

From the mid-19th century, many of the traditional uses of coppice woodland products died out as coal replaced firewood and charcoal as fuel. More recently, pressure-treated softwood fence posts from Eastern Europe have replaced local chestnut (hardwood) ones.

However, sweet chestnut from our coppiced woodland at Hurt Hill is used by National Trust properties all over the country for fencing. Off-cuts are used in wood-burners and our bio-mass boilers.

Endangered species

The loss of so much heath and ancient woodland over the last century has had a damaging effect on a wide range of species, especially heathland birds, reptiles and insects, some of which are now endangered.

Birds

Ground-nesting birds
Of the heathland birds, it is the ground-nesting species whose survival is most threatened by the loss of heathlands.

Woodlarks have richly patterned brown plumage and sing whilst in flight with a pretty, 'flutey' song. They are resident over much of Hindhead; some have even nested on the newly restored areas where the old A3 once stood.

Our commons are also home to nightjars. Slightly larger than woodlarks, these nocturnal birds with curiously long wings hawk for insects and moths. Their call rises and falls distinctively and is churning – or 'jarring' – giving them their name.

Dartford warblers
Dartford warblers nest in thick gorse rather than on the ground. The heathlands at Hindhead Common and the Devil's Punch Bowl are ideal for these delicate birds, but unusually for British species of warbler they remain resident all year. In harsh winters with periods of deep snow they are unable to forage and can starve. Dartford warblers once thrived in the Devil's Punch Bowl but recent sightings have been few after some difficult winters.

Other endangered species
Unlike birds, reptiles and insects cannot fly from one fragmented heathland area to another. This means colonies can easily become isolated and die out, risking the survival of rarer species. Conservationists are now trying to link heathland areas wherever possible, allowing struggling populations to migrate and re-establish in other areas if necessary.

Sand lizards
Of our native reptiles, it is the sand lizard which is most endangered; colonies at Hindhead had died out altogether before the National Trust started to restore the heathland. Sand lizards have been re-introduced to the Devil's Punch Bowl but, as it is very difficult to distinguish between them and common lizards, we are uncertain how successful this has been. However conditions at our commons are perfect for this reptile and efforts to establish a thriving colony will continue if necessary.

Silver-studded blue butterflies
As these butterflies lay their eggs in areas of heather of varying maturity, they are one of the most heathland-dependent and threatened insect species. There are established colonies at Frydinghurst, the southern corner of Hindhead Common.

Dormice
Dormice are a woodland mammals evident in our coppiced areas at Hurt Hill and Inval. They live almost entirely in deciduous trees, moving lithely from one to another. As they like to hibernate in recently coppiced stumps they have become endangered as coppicing has died out.

Images clockwise from top left

A male silver-studded blue butterfly. Despite their name, females are predominantly dark brown with orange spots

Sand lizards are usually dark but turn partly or wholly bright green in the mating season

Nightjars lay their eggs on bare soil, without a nest, among heather. Their mottled grey plumage offers useful camouflage before the chicks hatch

Dormice sometimes hibernate for six months of the year

In the winter of 1962/3, the British population of Dartford warblers dropped to just 10 pairs

Centre The scientific name for woodlarks is 'Lullula' after their call, which sounds like 'lu-lu-lu'

The A3 Tunnel

In the 1990s–2012, the Portsmouth Road returned to centre stage.

Traffic and tail-backs

The years following 1945 saw motorised traffic increase dramatically. Having become virtually deserted after the railway was completed, the Portsmouth Road, by now known as the A3, suffered constant heavy traffic which cut Hindhead Common off from the Devil's Punch Bowl.

By the mid-1990s, road improvements along the A3 left Hindhead the only bottleneck between London and Portsmouth. Daily tailbacks stretching round the Devil's Punch Bowl blighted the area.

A solution had to be found. But, as earlier generations had discovered, going round Hindhead is no easier than going over it. Various new routes were suggested but were discounted due to cost, local objections or because they would necessitate the destruction of conservation-grade countryside.

Got to go through it

Finally the scheme for the A3 tunnel was proposed in 1993. This option overcame almost everyone's objections, despite its considerable cost, but it posed a dilemma for the National Trust. The proposed plan would mean losing 20 acres of land at Nutcombe and a further three acres below Gibbet Hill, but Sir Robert Hunter's National Trust Act prohibits us from parting with our property (see page 13).

However, in some circumstances, we are able to exchange land of comparable quality. The tunnel scheme not only offered to compensate us with land near Boundless Lane and at Highcombe Edge, but also, crucially, to close and remove the A3 round the Devil's Punch Bowl. Appreciating the enormous benefits for Hindhead, we supported the project.

Another feat of engineering

Following a public inquiry which recommended in the scheme's favour, the

project was given the go-ahead by the government in October 2006.

Preliminary work to minimise disruption to wildlife, particularly the dormice near the site of the northern portals, started in January 2007 and tunnelling began in February 2008. In July 2011, on time and on budget, the tunnel opened and simultaneously the road round the Punch Bowl was closed. For the first time in years, the roar of traffic, the fumes and the tailbacks had gone.

More challenges ahead

For us this was just the beginning of one of the most ambitious projects we have ever undertaken on an open-space property: re-uniting Hindhead Common with the Devil's Punch Bowl. Within days, the contractor, Balfour Beatty, brought in heavy machinery to break up the old road and re-contour the hillside. Tarmac planings were buried deeply in the old road cuttings before sandstone material extracted from the tunnelling process was brought back to cover the scars.

The whole process took ten months. On 15 March 2012, the then-Director General of the National Trust, Dame Fiona Reynolds, came to Hindhead to celebrate the return of the land on which the Portsmouth Road had stood for over 180 years.

Above The A3 Tunnel

Opposite The Portsmouth road before (above) and after (below) the construction of the A3 tunnel. No longer a route for vehicles, it is now growing over and a popular walk

Re-uniting the commons

Two major tasks remained before the heathlands across Hindhead Common and the Devil's Punch Bowl could be considered integrated: establishing heathland flora on the re-landscaped hillside, and creating wide heathland corridors to connect the commons.

Encouraging heathland flora

The sandy material used to bury the road had a natural acidity which would support heathland plants, but coming from deep under the hillside, it had no natural seed-base. So seed-laden heather and grass clippings harvested from Hindhead Common were scattered over the newly re-contoured areas. We used clippings rather than pure seed because test germination sites had shown these were more likely to be successful.

Major scrub clearance

To minimise the visual impact of the continuous heavy traffic, we had encouraged dense scrub to grow either side of the road. Unfortunately this acted as a barrier between the two commons for reptiles and insects, while birds, put off by noise and fumes, did not nest within 200 yards of the road.

By autumn 2012 we had secured the agreement of Natural England and the Forestry Commission to embark on the second task: a major programme to drastically thin, and in some places clear fell, the densest parts of the scrub and immature pine, which was between the between the old A3 (Byway 500). This work reconnects the heathlands, enabling reptiles and insects to migrate and re-establish in adjoining heathland habitats if necessary.

A big reveal

Our efforts have not just benefitted rare species. Long-lost views have re-emerged, including the vistas from the byway across the Punch Bowl valley, restoring its invigorating feeling of wildness and space.

New adventures

We have marked out some interesting new self-guided walks on both commons.

The **Highcombe Hike** sets off northwards from the main car park along Highcombe Ridge, before descending into the Punch Bowl and returning along the 'Sailors' Lane'.

Hidden Hindhead is a longer route passing the Sailor's Stone, Celtic Cross and the remains of Lord Pirrie's belvedere.

A work in progress

Although our two precious commons are now properly connected, it will still be a few years and a lot of hard work before the restored heathland is fully established.

Closure of the A3 round the Punch Bowl has allowed us to re-create the wilderness which once made these hills so treacherous, and whose clean air and spectacular scenery later attracted a generation of writers and inspired Sir Robert Hunter to save it for the nation.

It also makes it possible to walk the four miles from Haslemere to Thursley without crossing a road.

Hopefully the environmental benefits of this incredible project will ensure that silver-studded blue butterflies and sand lizards thrive all along this stunning heathland route.

Above The waymark logos for the Highcombe Hike (left) and Hidden Hindhead (right) walking routes

Left Walkers on the old A3 road (Byway 500)

The A3D Project

A3D Hindhead was a community project to celebrate the reunited landscape. It tells the story of the A3 road through scultural (3D) landmarks.

The project was initiated by local resident Denise McCullough, who suggested a permanent creative legacy to celebrate both the unified landscape and the feat of engineering that provided the tunnel at Hindhead. Her vision was for children from local schools to contribute while exploring and understanding their local heritage. Her idea was supported by the National Trust, Balfour Beatty, Haslemere Educational Museum and Cultural Shift; the Heritage Lottery Fund awarded the project a generous grant.

Heritage: the carved benches

It was decided to produce a number of images influenced by Hindhead's landscape, literature, history, wildlife and tunnel scheme. Working alongside sculptor Ruth Wheeler, each school developed one theme into designs which the children then carved onto locally-sourced oak panels. These now form a circle of benches near the main viewpoint over the Punch Bowl.

Legacy: a free-form sculpture

Sculptor Jon Edgar worked with another team of children on a 'legacy' sculpture. Edgar decided to create this on site and in November 2012 a three-ton piece of Portland stone was delivered to Hindhead. The children sketched up the block with images; over 45 days of freezing mid-winter weather, Edgar carved out these images while

encouraging the group's continuous input. The sculpture had no pre-conceived design but gradually forms emerged that reflect many features of Hindhead's history and scenery.

It now sits on a plinth placed on grassland once occupied by the old A3.

Below The completed legacy sculpture, which has been named 'Portal'